PRAYERS &
PROCLAMATIONS

PRAYERS &
PROCLAMATIONS

Derek
PRINCE

WHITAKER
HOUSE

Publisher's Note: This book was compiled from a previous editions of *The Power of Proclamation* and *Prayers and Proclamations* with additional materials from the extensive archive of Derek Prince's unpublished materials and edited by the Derek Prince Ministries editorial team.

PRAYERS AND PROCLAMATIONS
Revised and Expanded Edition

Derek Prince Ministries
P.O. Box 19501
Charlotte, North Carolina 28219
www.derekprince.org

ISBN: 978-1-60374-122-4
Printed in the United States of America
© 1990, 2010 by Derek Prince Ministries, International

Whitaker House
1030 Hunt Valley Circle
New Kensington, PA 15068
www.whitakerhouse.com

3 4 5 6 7 8 9 10 11 12 **UU** 18 17 16 15 14 13 12 11

Contents

Proclaiming God's Word

1. Proclaiming the Word..............................9

2. What It Means to Proclaim..................11

3. Multiplying the Power
   of Communication..............................15

4. The Rod of Moses.................................19

5. Taking Hold of God's Word.................23

6. The Word and the Spirit Together......27

7. Learning to Tremble at God's Word...33

8. Executing God's Judgment..................37

9. Exercising Authority..........................41

10. Overcoming Negative Thinking.........43

11. Protection through Proclamation.......47

12. Financial and Physical Needs.............51

13. Proclamation in National and
    International Affairs.........................55

14. Concerning Christianity
    and Opposing Forces........................59

Proclamations

15. How to Utilize these Declarations......67

16. The Fear of the Lord.............................. 73

17. Righteousness and Holiness................ 79

18. Health and Strength............................. 91

19. Guidance, Protection,
    and Preservation................................. 99

20. God's Intervention in
    Human Affairs 109

21. Testing and Trials 119

22. Spiritual Conflict 127

23. Perfect Redemption 133

24. Mental and Emotional Stability 141

25. Serving God.. 147

26. The Divine Exchange......................... 157

27. Confession for Overcomers
    (Let the Redeemed Say So) 159

28. By This I Overcome the Devil........... 161

29. Declaration of Confidence
    in God's Protection........................... 163

30. Proclamations on Behalf of Israel..... 165

31. Twelve Steps to a Good Year............. 169

Scripture Index 177

About the Author 183

PROCLAIMING GOD'S WORD

Chapter One

Proclaiming the Word

Tremendous power is released through proclaiming the Word of God. Many believers are unaware of this amazing potential that is available to all Christians. Whether it is a situation of personal need or an international crisis that needs to be resolved, learning how to proclaim the Word of God into that situation releases God's creative power, which can utterly transform the circumstances. Every believer has both the privilege and the responsibility to proclaim God's Word.

Throughout my years of ministry, whenever my wife, Ruth, was with me, I would always begin my messages by inviting her to join me in making a proclamation. God taught us to begin in this way, and we discovered that proclaiming the Word in faith at the beginning of a meeting made a tremendous difference in the spiritual atmosphere in the meeting and in the anointing on the speaker.

One of my favorite proclamations from Scripture is one we used frequently—and one that, in many ways, sums up the message of this book.

For as the rain comes down, and the snow from heaven, and do not return there, but water the earth, and make it bring forth and bud, that it may give seed to the sower and bread to the eater, so shall My word be that goes forth from My mouth; it shall not return to Me void, but it shall accomplish what I please, and it shall prosper in the thing for which I sent it. (Isaiah 55:10–11)

Chapter Two

What It Means to Proclaim

The word *proclaim* is a strong word. It comes from a Latin word that means "to shout forth." A related word in the language of the New Testament is one that means "to confess." *Confess* means "to say the same as." For us, as believers in the Bible, confession involves saying the same thing with our mouths as God has already said in His Word. When we make the words of our mouths agree with the Word of God, we position ourselves to receive the full backing and authority of Jesus.

In Hebrews 3:1, the writer said that Jesus is the *"High Priest of our confession."* This is a very important statement. If we have no confession, we have no High Priest. Jesus is the High Priest of what we confess. In other words, whenever we say with our mouths what the Bible says about us as believers in Christ, then we have Jesus as our High Priest in heaven, releasing His authority and His blessing over our confession.

If we remain silent, however, in a certain sense, we cut off His ministry to us as High Priest. If we make a wrong confession, we do even worse. In such a case, we invite negative forces to surround us and move upon us.

A proclamation is a confession that is made aggressive. It is a word that speaks of spiritual warfare. It is releasing the authority of God's Word into a situation, into your own life, your family, the life of your church, a political situation, or whatever it may be. There are countless situations that need to have the power of God released into them, and there is no more effective way to release the power of God than by proclamation.

Proclaiming is really the activity of a herald. *Herald* is a word we don't use very much today, but in medieval times, the herald was a person with authority from a king, a duke, or some other nobleman who would go to a public place and make a proclamation of the will and decision of that ruler. He would shout out, "Oyez, Oyez!" and then make the proclamation.

So, whenever people heard "Oyez, Oyez," they knew it represented the voice of authority. They would stand at attention and listen to what was being said. In the New Testament, although it doesn't clearly come out in most translations, the word *preach* is the word for a herald. It means "to proclaim."

Chapter Three

Multiplying the Power of Communication

These days, through the use of modern communication technology, we can proclaim God's Word far more widely than was ever possible before. I have been a Bible teacher for many decades, and I always felt my duty was to interpret the Bible—to explain it and help people to understand it.

Many years ago, the Lord began to impress on me the word *proclaim*. I felt that He was challenging me to go beyond teaching His Word and to begin proclaiming it. The result was the beginning of my radio Bible teaching ministry, which started on eight stations in the U.S. in 1979 and was eventually translated into more than thirteen languages, effectively covering most of the globe.

Essentially, it is a ministry of proclamation. The key verse that stirred me to establish the radio ministry was Matthew 24:14:

> *This gospel of the kingdom will be preached in all the world as a witness to all the nations, and then the end will come.* (Matthew 24:14)

This age cannot close until we have done our job as the church of Jesus Christ—as His witnesses on the earth. Our task is to proclaim the gospel *"in all the world as a witness to all the nations."* I have learned by experience the tremendous power of the Word of God simply proclaimed in faith. It accomplishes the most marvelous results.

I remember the story of an American woman who was everything a woman shouldn't be, by Christian standards. She was a Marxist, a feminist, and a lesbian. She found herself in a small ship on the South China Sea with some of her companions as a storm was coming up. The others said, "Go down below and turn on the radio. See what you can find out about the weather."

She turned on the radio and just happened to catch my radio program, which was being broadcast from Manila in the Philippines. She heard enough to get saved right then and there. As a result, she became just as radical the other way—radical for God. It was not just the teaching that she heard; it was simply the Word proclaimed that did its work.

Chapter Four

The Rod of Moses

Look at the example of Moses when God called him to go back and be the deliverer of Israel out of Egypt. You may remember that God appeared to him in the burning bush and, in Exodus 4, said that He was sending Moses back to Egypt in order to deliver Israel from bondage. Despite God's commission, Moses felt he was not equipped for the task. Moses had lost all of the self-confidence he had had at the age of forty—he was now eighty. He said, in effect, "Why me, Lord? I can't do anything. How can I do it?"

In His ever-practical way, God said to Moses, *"What is that in your hand?"* (Exodus 4:2).

"It's a rod," Moses replied. What he held was a rod like any other shepherd would carry. He didn't think there was anything particularly special about his rod.

God proceeded to demonstrate to Moses the miraculous potential in that seemingly insignificant rod. At one point, the Lord said, *"Cast it on the ground"* (Exodus 4:3). When Moses did, it became a snake, and he ran away from it. Then God said, *"Reach out your hand and take it by the tail"* (verse 4). Anyone who deals with snakes will tell you that one should never pick up a snake by the tail. But Moses obeyed God, and the snake became a rod once again. In doing this, God showed Moses how to use the rod as an instrument of divine authority. With that rod, Moses defeated the magicians of Egypt, stripped Pharaoh of his power, humiliated their gods, and brought Israel out of Egypt—from slavery to freedom.

If you analyze the rest of the book of Exodus from there on, the entire deliverance of Israel out of Egypt was achieved by that rod. Every time Moses wanted God to intervene, he stretched out his rod, and God intervened. Moses' authority was symbolized by the rod in his hand. When the Red Sea needed to be divided so that Israel could pass through, Moses stretched out his rod, and the waters split apart.

When the Egyptians were crossing the seabed in pursuit of the children of Israel, Moses put forth his rod again, and the waters swallowed them up. The only equipment Moses needed for the entire task that God had called him to was that simple shepherd's rod—the very thing he didn't think held any significance when he first held it in his hand.

Chapter 5

Taking Hold of
God's Word

You, too, have a rod in your hand: your
Bible. If you can understand its unlimited
potential, you can use it as Moses used his
rod: to extend God's authority into any situation
where Satan opposes the people and the
purposes of God.

Over our years together, my wife, Ruth,
and I fought a continuing war against Satan,
who opposed us and our ministry in many
different ways. I sensed that one of his goals
was to kill Ruth. In this war, the Holy Spirit
taught us how to take hold of the Bible as
our rod and extend God's authority through
it into every area where Satan was opposing
us.

The Holy Spirit led us systematically to
Scripture after Scripture, and showed us how
to direct them to each area of attack. The
strategy the Holy Spirit taught us was:

Proclamation!
Thanksgiving!
Praise!

First, *proclaim* the appropriate Scripture with bold, unwavering confidence. To make this fully effective, we often personalized the passages we quoted, making any grammatical substitutions needed to apply the verses more personally to ourselves. For instance, where the Bible says, "you," we changed it in our proclamation to "I," "we," or "us."[1]

Second, we accepted the Scripture we proclaimed as true, even before we saw its actual outworking in any situation. The natural result of this was to *thank* God for it.

This logically led to the third step: loud, jubilant *praise*.

In Song of Solomon 6:4, Solomon describes Christ's bride, the church, as *"awesome as an army with banners."* Under these banners— Proclamation, Thanksgiving, and Praise— Ruth and I were able to drive out the hosts of darkness and enter into the freedom that

---

[1] Editor's note: You will notice these types of changes to the exact wording of Scripture through the Proclamations section.

God had appointed for us as His believing people.

Unless otherwise indicated, we use the *New King James Version*. Where we have felt it appropriate to make significant changes in the wording, this has been indicated by an asterisk (*).

The proclamations and prayers will be grouped under ten headings.

Fear of the Lord

Righteousness and Holiness

Health and Strength

Guidance, Protection, and Preservation

God's Intervention in Human Affairs

Testing and Trials

Spiritual Conflict

Perfect Redemption

Mental and Emotional Stability

Serving God

Finally, at the end, there are six comprehensive proclamations that were special favorites of ours.

In order to receive the maximum benefit from these Scriptures, here are three simple steps to follow:

1. Ask the Holy Spirit to make "alive" to you any Scriptures that are appropriate to your particular situation.

2. Read these Scriptures through many times—out loud, if possible.

3. Gradually proceed from reading aloud to systematic memorization. This is a natural step. The Hebrew expression for "to learn by heart" actually means "to learn by mouth." As you read the words aloud, they gradually become imprinted on your memory.

Before we get started, however, let me share with you some of the truths I've learned about proclaiming God's Word.

Chapter Six

The Word and the Spirit Together

As we noted about Moses at the beginning of the previous chapter, if you are a Bible-believing, committed Christian, you also have a rod in your hand. It is the Word of God. Think of your Bible as the only instrument you need in your hand to be able to do everything God calls you to do.

The first thing we need to realize is the power of God's Word. It is a supernatural book. Just like Moses' rod, it contains power that isn't obvious when you first look at it. But when you begin to understand it, its power is actually limitless.

Let me give you a few Scriptures that reveal the power of the Word of God:

> *By the word of the LORD were the heavens made; and all the host of them by the breath of his mouth.*
>
> (Psalm 33:6 KJV)

The Hebrew word for "breath" is *ruach*, which is also the word for "spirit." Thus, all of creation came about through two agents: the Word of God and the Spirit of God. Everything that exists, has existed, or will exist owes its origin to these two forces working together. The Word must work with the Spirit. I think that might be why it was translated as *breath* and not as *spirit*.

Think about the tremendous power of words, and yet how simple they can be. When I was teaching English as a second language to African students, I had to learn elementary phonetics. I made some interesting discoveries about words. How do we actually speak? As we release breath out of our lungs, it passes through the mouth and nose, and the various alterations it is subjected to determine the sound of the words that come out. Because of this, you cannot speak without breathing.

This is a picture of how God speaks, too. Every time He speaks a word, it is carried by His breath—His Spirit. The Word and the Spirit of God always go together. The Word and the Spirit of God brought the universe into being, and they continue working together to sustain it.

There is a very powerful Scripture in 2 Peter that tells us three facts: the Word creates, the Word maintains, and the Word abolishes.

> *By the word of God the heavens were of old, and the earth standing out of water and in the water, by which the world that then existed perished, being flooded with water. But the heavens and the earth which are now preserved by the same word, are reserved for fire until the day of judgment and perdition of ungodly men.* (2 Peter 3:5–7)

By the Word of God, the earth and heavens were brought into being; by the Word of God, they are maintained in being; and by the Word of God, and in His timing, they will pass away. The Word of God creates, maintains, and abolishes. Sometimes, when I look at the mess that man is making of this planet, I am glad that the Word of God will abolish this mess one day. God accomplishes all these things by His Word.

Let us return to the Scripture quoted at the beginning: Isaiah 55:10–11. This word must come out of God's mouth, otherwise it is not effective.

For as the rain comes down, and the snow from heaven, and do not return there, but water the earth, and make it bring forth and bud, that it may give seed to the sower and bread to the eater, so shall My word be that goes forth from My mouth; it shall not return to me void, but it shall accomplish what I please, and it shall prosper in the thing for which I sent it.

Notice that God said, *"My word...that goes forth from My mouth."* In other words, "My word, when it is propelled by My breath."

In 2 Corinthians 3:6, Paul said, *"The letter kills, but the Spirit gives life."* In other words, the Word by itself, without the breath, does not bring life. It has to be the Word and the Spirit together. You may have a sermon that has a lot of Scripture in it, but if it does not have the breath of the Spirit, then it is dry. It does not produce life; it produces death. The two must always operate together.

I want to draw a parallel with the experience of Moses to see how we can make the Word of God effective by proclaiming it. By proclaiming it, I mean releasing it into a particular situation. It takes confidence and boldness. It is not for the timid; you must make up your mind that you believe it.

It is God's Word, and if you say it with a believing heart through believing lips, it is just as effective when His Spirit says it through you as it is when God Himself says it. If the Spirit of God propels the Word of God through your mouth, it is as effective as when God spoke the universe into being.

Chapter Seven

Learning to Tremble at God's Word

We begin this chapter with the recognition that the first thing that happened to Moses was that he became frightened. When Moses threw the rod on the ground, it became a snake, and he ran from it. Like Moses, before we can be effective in proclaiming, we must learn to have a healthy fear of the Word of God. We have to learn to tremble at the Word of God.

> *Thus says the LORD: "Heaven is My throne, and earth is My footstool. Where is the house that you will build Me? And where is the place of My rest? For all those things My hand has made, and all those things exist," says the LORD. "But on this one will I look: on him who is poor and of a contrite spirit, and who trembles at My word."* (Isaiah 66:1–2)

We can't build anything that will impress God because He has already created the entire universe. There is one thing, however, that does attract His favor: *"On this one will I look* [esteem or respect]*."* Whom will God respect and take into account? *"Him who is poor and of a contrite spirit and who trembles at My word."*

So, like Moses, our first reaction must be fear and awe at the Word of God. There is far too little fear of the Word of God in the church today. Perhaps we have become too familiar with it. We quote it and bandy it about, but too many fail to show true reverence for it. This attitude must change.

Let me give you two reasons why we should tremble before the Word of God. The first is when Jesus said:

If anyone hears My words and does not believe [receive them]*, I do not judge him; for I did not come to judge the world but to save the world. He who rejects Me, and does not receive My words, has that which judges him; the word that I have spoken will judge him in the last day.* (John 12:47–48)

One day, we will all be judged by the Word of God. Imagine yourself standing before almighty God, having to give an account for your life, as I believe we all must do one day. I think you would tremble; you would be very concerned. Jesus said that we should have the same attitude toward the Word of God because it will be our judge on that day. Every time we open the pages of the Bible and read it, if we can understand this, we are looking at that which will one day judge us. No wonder we should tremble at it.

Then, Jesus made another amazing statement:

> *If anyone loves Me, he will keep My word; and My Father will love him, and We will come to him and make Our home with him.* (John 14:23)

This is one of the few places in the Bible where the plural pronoun is used to describe God. *"We* [Father and Son] *will come to him."* How will they come? It will be through God's Word. In other words, when we open up to His Word, then God Himself—the Father and the

Son—is coming into our lives, willing to make His home with us.

Imagine a vision in which you actually saw the Lord Jesus coming into your home. You would be overwhelmed; you would have a sense of awe. You would want to fall at His feet in reverence. Here, Jesus is saying, "Not only will I come, but the Father will come, as well." And They will come through the Word of God.

Most of us in the contemporary church need a change of attitude regarding God's Word. We need to show a much greater sense of reverence, awe, and fear. The Word won't be effective in our lives in the way I have described until we learn to reverence that Word.

Chapter Eight

Executing God's Judgment

The previous chapter showed us the importance of trembling at the Word. This is the first thing that happened to Moses. He suddenly realized the power that was present in his rod, and he ran from it. The second thing he did was to take hold of the rod. By faith, he gripped it and the snake became a rod in his hand once again. So, after we have trembled, we need to take hold of God's Word.

The last four verses of Psalm 149 speak powerfully to this.

Let the saints be joyful in glory; let them sing aloud on their beds. Let the high praises of God be in their mouth, and a two-edged sword in their hand, to execute vengeance on the nations, and punishments on the peoples; to bind their kings with chains, and their nobles with fetters of iron; to execute on

*them the written judgment; this honor
have all His saints. Praise the LORD!*
(Psalm 149:5–9)

The saints spoken of here are all true, dedicated believers—people who tremble at the sound of the Word of God but are totally committed to it. And there is an amazing series of statements given. Can you identify yourself as belonging to the saints? If you have the high praises of God in your mouth and a two-edged sword in your hand, then you can execute judgment on the nations. Can you begin to see yourself, by faith, as part of this scenario? This honor or privilege belongs to all the saints. What an awesome responsibility! I think the way each of us prays would be quite different if we were to really see ourselves in the light of these verses.

Notice that we are *"to execute...the written judgment."* Where is that judgment written? It is in the Word. We are not the ones to make those judgments; God has made them. But we have the privilege of executing those judgments on the nations and their rulers. In other words, believers have a unique and important part to play in history.

The tragedy is that so many Christians are so far from understanding all God has made available to us, not to mention all He expects from us. I want to emphasize that we don't make the judgments; we find the judgments in the written Word of God. Our role is to execute them.

How do we do this? We do it by proclaiming from the Word of God the judgments that are written there. We simply proclaim them; we are the heralds. We stand in the marketplace of the world and shout out, "Oyez, Oyez!" Then we announce the decree of God.

Chapter Nine

Exercising Authority

As we come to the next stage, I want to be very practical and down-to-earth. After Moses grasped the rod, what did he do next? When he got back to Egypt, he stretched it out. By doing so, he exercised the authority that was in the rod. I want to suggest that we need to do the same. We need to take the written Word of God and stretch it out in any situation where the authority of God is needed.

One of the most effective ways to release the power of God into a situation is by proclaiming it in faith and under the anointing of the Holy Spirit. Remember that the Word must go with the breath. When the breath, or Spirit, of God propels His Word from our mouths, we can release it into a situation. And those words have all the authority of almighty God in that situation.

God did not step down off His throne, take the rod from Moses, and say, "I'll do it for you." That seems to be what many of us expect to happen. But God says, in effect, "You've got the rod; you do it!" Although it was actually called *"the rod of God"* in Exodus 4:20, Moses was the one who held it and wielded it.

I am going to address a number of situations that need the rod of God. I will begin with matters that are personal and then move on to needs that are regional, national, and even international. I want to highlight the different ways in which we can stretch out the rod. These will all be proclamations used regularly in my devotional times with the Lord. (Often, these times were anything but quiet times!) I'm not suggesting that there is any more power if you shout—it all depends on how the Holy Spirit leads you at the time. Over a period of years, I have gathered between one and two hundred proclamations that I have made on a regular basis. Some of these I have proclaimed hundreds of times.

Chapter Ten

Overcoming Negative Thinking

Remember—especially if you have a lot of negative thinking and speaking in your background—just saying one of these proclamations once is not going to have much of an impact. These proclamations need to be spoken out loud over and over for real change to come from the heavenly realm. You need to go on speaking them out loud until they become part of your thinking.

You may know that I am from England and that British people can be pretty negative. We tend to be, by nature, pessimists. I myself was the pessimist of pessimists! Thankfully, God gradually revolutionized me, but it took Him a long while!

Whenever I faced a difficult situation, I automatically began to think of all the trouble and bad things that could happen. Maybe you have the same problem.

I would use the weapon of the Word in many different ways. In Jeremiah 29:11, God says to Israel, *"I know the plans that I have for you...plans for good and not for evil"* (TLB). Other translations say, *"plans to prosper you"* (NIV) and *"not for calamity to give you a future and a hope"* (NASB).

Every time I found myself beginning to entertain a negative picture or thought, I would say, "Lord, I thank You that You know the plans You have for me, plans of good and not of evil, plans of prosperity and not of calamity, to give me a future and a hope."

I may have had to say it several times, but in the end, the negative atmosphere dissipated, and I had a strong, confident, positive attitude. If you start to say this at the beginning of the day, you will have a good day—you will accomplish the things you set out to do.

Your attitude makes a huge difference in the way other people treat you. If you walk into a store with a positive attitude, the staff will help you. If you go in expecting bad service, discourtesy, or trouble, you will probably get them.

I think it is always good to personalize the proclamations that you make. So, when the Bible says "you," replace it with "I." By doing this, you are saying, "This applies to me."

Let's start with self-defense. Suppose you are attacked by a lot of fearful, negative thoughts and you find yourself continually thinking about what would happen if you were to die. Perhaps you need surgery, and the doctor says he can't guarantee you will come through it. Ruth and I faced this scenario when she was ill. Here is a Scripture we must have used thousands of times: *"I shall not die, but live, and declare the works of the LORD"* (Psalm 118:17).

Chapter Eleven

Protection through Proclamation

Suppose people are speaking or even pray-ing against you. Your remedy is Isaiah 54:17, on which the following proclamation is based:

> No weapon that is formed against me shall prosper, and every tongue which rises against me in judgment I do con-demn. This is my heritage as a servant of the LORD, and my righteousness is from You, O LORD of Hosts.

Ruth and I used to say this every night before going to sleep. When we confess that our righteousness is from the Lord, this is the reason we can condemn the tongues that ac-cuse us. It is because they are refusing God's righteousness and that always means being on the losing side.

I would like to make clear, too, that we would say, "If there are those who speak against us or are seeking evil for us, we for-give them. And having forgiven them, we bless them in the name of the Lord." We would always seek to replace the negative with the positive.

The Bible says that if people curse us, we should not curse them back but rather bless them. Paul said, *"Do not be overcome by evil, but overcome evil with good"* (Romans 12:21). Goodness is the only power strong enough to overcome evil.

When we were attacked, we would use a proclamation from Deuteronomy 33:25–27(NIV):

> The bolts of our gates will be iron and bronze, and our strength will equal your days. There is no one like the God of Jeshurun, who rides on the heavens to help you and on the clouds in His majesty. The eternal God is our refuge, and underneath are the everlasting arms. He will drive out our enemy be-fore us, saying, "Destroy him!"

That kind of proclamation really fright-ens Satan. Remember that our battle is not against flesh and blood but against spiritual powers of wickedness in heavenly realms. (See Ephesians 6:12.) The weapons God provides are very powerful, but they must be used in the right context.

Chapter Twelve

Financial and Physical Needs

You may have various kinds of need—financial or physical, for instance. For financial needs, we have used 2 Corinthians 9:8. Again, we have changed a few of the words, but basically it is from the King James Version:

> *God is able to make all grace abound toward us; that we, always having all sufficiency in all things, may abound to every good work.*

It all starts with three simple words: *"God is able."* Then it says what He is able to do. In this amazing verse, the word *"all"* occurs five times (once as *"always"* and once as *"every"*), and the word *"abound"* occurs twice. It would hardly be possible to get more abundance into one verse! It is all grace. And how is grace received? *"By grace you have been saved through faith"* (Ephesians 2:8). It is not something we earn or deserve. It does not depend on our social standing. We receive everything by faith in God's grace. This verse is the financial foundation of our ministry.

Then, suppose you are faced with something challenging that you think you can't do. You don't have the education, the physical strength, the discernment—whatever it is that the situation seems to require. In such circumstances, we would resort to Philippians 4:13. This is the "Prince version." I know Greek, and I think the Lord has given me a good rendering of the language in order to bring out the meaning better than any other version I know of: "I can do all things through the one who empowers me within."

I use the word *empower* because the Greek word is from *dunamis*, which is normally translated "power." So, there is a source of power within you that is released by your proclamation. Even if you don't have the education, the strength, or the discernment to do something, when it is a task assigned by the will of God, there is One inside you who empowers you from within.

You may be afflicted by sickness of some kind. One of our favorite verses dealing with healing is 1 Peter 2:24:

> Jesus Himself bore our sins in His own body on the tree, that we, having died to sins, might live for righteousness; by whose wounds we were healed.

Notice, it is expressed in the past tense. When the Bible speaks about healing in the atonement, the future tense is never used. Seven hundred years before Jesus came, Isaiah said, *"By His stripes we **are** healed"* (Isaiah 53:5, emphasis added). After the atoning death and resurrection of Christ, looking back, Peter said, "By whose wounds we were healed."

That gives you a completely different perspective. It doesn't mean that you automatically cease to be sick, but it gives you a different basis on which to encounter and challenge sickness. Sometimes you will have to keep confessing it over and over for a long time. But you must decide which is more reliable—God's Word or your symptoms.

Chapter Thirteen

Proclamation in National and International Affairs

Now we move to an area where a more aggressive approach is necessary. I want to deal with intervention in national and international affairs. Ruth and I used to spend a lot of time praying outside our own personal needs for all kinds of situations, including the destinies of nations. Here are some Scriptures that will encourage and help you to do the same.

One of our favorites is a combination of Daniel 2:20–22 and Daniel 4:34–35. The first words were spoken by Daniel and the second by Nebuchadnezzar, but the message is the same.

Blessed be the name of God for ever and ever, for wisdom and might are His. And He changes the times and the seasons; He removes kings and raises up kings;

> *He gives wisdom to the wise and knowl-*
> *edge to those who have understanding.*
> *He reveals deep and secret things; He*
> *knows what is in the darkness, and the*
> *light dwells with Him....For His do-*
> *minion is an everlasting dominion, and*
> *His kingdom is from generation to gen-*
> *eration. All the inhabitants of the earth*
> *are reputed as nothing; He does accord-*
> *ing to His will in the army of heaven*
> *and among the inhabitants of the earth.*
> *No one can restrain His hand or say to*
> *Him, "What have You done?"*

Remember that the second section of those words came from a ruler who had recently been an unbeliever. That should encourage us that God can indeed change the hearts of evil rulers if we learn how to pray.

Then there are two passages from 2 Chronicles. They are both single-verse prayers, and we would often speak them aloud to get us going before focusing on praying more for the specific aspects of the particular situation at hand.

LORD, there is no one like You to help the powerless against the mighty. Help us, O LORD our God, for we rely on You, and in Your name we have come against this vast army. O LORD, You are our God; do not let man prevail against You. (2 Chronicles 14:11 NIV)

The second one is 2 Chronicles 20:6:

O LORD, God of our fathers, are You not the God who is in heaven? You rule over all the kingdoms of the earth. Power and might are in Your hand, and no one can withstand You. (NIV)

Now look at Psalm 33:8–12, which is a tremendously powerful affirmation whenever you are dealing with a world situation:

Let all the earth fear the LORD; let all the inhabitants of the world stand in awe of Him. For He spoke, and it was done; He commanded, and it stood fast. The LORD brings the counsel of the nations to nothing; He makes the plans of the peoples of no effect. The counsel of the LORD stands forever, the plans of

*His heart to all generations. Blessed is
the nation whose God is the LORD, and
the people He has chosen as His own
inheritance.* (Psalm 33:8–12)

In other words, "Who is going to come out
of it all as a winner?" The nation whose God
is the Lord. All the plans of governments, nations, the United Nations, and so on are just
nonsense if they are contrary to the plans of
God.

Chapter Fourteen

Concerning Christianity and Opposing Forces

Finally, I want to look at some verses that relate specifically to Israel, which is one of the areas we have prayed about most over the years. You may not have exactly the same burden, but you can take the principles and apply them in your particular situation.

The regions of the world that are now often referred to as the "10/40 Window" have proven to be among the hardest to penetrate with the truth of the gospel. These are countries that are found between ten and forty degrees north of the equator, areas considered to have the greatest socioeconomic problems. I believe there is a very important reason for this that actually underlines the impact that proclamation can have.

You probably know that five times a day, every day, from every Muslim mosque in the world, a proclamation goes forth: "There is no God but Allah, and Mohammed is his prophet." This proclamation has been going out every day for more than 1,400 years. You don't have to do the math to realize that this proclamation has gone out billions of times over the centuries. Perhaps this helps us to understand why there is such a strong religious power over this entire region. What is the cause of this? I believe it has much to do with the power of that proclamation.

This principle applies no matter whether the proclamation is positive or negative. In order to overcome the accumulated power of negative proclamations, we have to make positive proclamations to counter them. If you think that this is a hopeless task, remember the situation when Moses and Aaron were confronted by the Egyptian magicians. When Aaron threw down his rod on the ground and it became a snake, the magicians did the same, but Aaron's snake ate up all of the snakes of the Egyptian magicians. (See Exodus 7:10–12.) Our proclamations can overcome every negative proclamation if we know how to make them.

Now I want to look at two biblical proclamations specifically in regard to Israel and her land. The first is Psalm 125:3:

The scepter of the wicked will not remain over the land allotted to the righteous. (NIV)

In this context, the *"scepter of the wicked"* is represented by any force that is opposed to God—His peoples and His purposes. You will have to speak out this verse in faith, especially when everything seems to be exactly the opposite. In fact, that's the best time to say it! You are stretching out your rod of authority, and your rod (or snake) is going to eat up all the snakes of the magicians.

The second proclamation regarding Israel is Psalm 129:5–6:

Let them all be confounded and turned back that hate Zion. Let them be as the grass upon the housetops, which withers before it grows up. (KJV)

I serve notice on all those who hate Zion that they will never grow to full maturity;

they will wither before they are fully grown. That is the Word of God, and it is going to come to pass.

Let me give you one more passage about the restoration of Israel.

Sing with gladness for Jacob, and shout among the chief of the nations; proclaim, give praise, and say, "O LORD, save Your people, the remnant of Israel!"

(Jeremiah 31:7)

Look at the verbs in that verse: sing, shout, proclaim, give praise, and say. These are all specific actions that we can be involved in. The word *proclaim* is right in there, as well. Then it says in verse 10:

Hear the word of the LORD, O nations, and declare it in the isles afar off, and say, "He who scattered Israel will gather him, and keep him as a shepherd does his flock."

This is something we can proclaim, or declare, over all the nations—especially those in the "10/40 Window." The same God who scattered Israel is now gathering them once again. As God's people, we can have a part to play in proclaiming the truth of God's Word until it becomes a reality.

PROCLAMATIONS

Chapter Fifteen

How to Utilize These Declarations

To begin this section, I want to give you some guidelines on how to apply these proclamations that Ruth and I used both publicly and privately over the twenty years of our marriage.

These proclamations are arranged by category to help you use them appropriately. There are more than one hundred of them. So if you wanted to use one every day, there would be enough for four months. Then you could start all over again.

As an example, let's look at a combination of proclamations entitled A Declaration of Confidence in God's Protection (which also appears again at the end of the book). Ruth and I made this declaration on a regular bases and found it to be of tremendous benefit in our lives.

Many testimonies have been received over the years from people sharing how they have been set free and have experienced a greater sense of God's presence as they have proclaimed the truths contained in this proclamation.

I encourage you to take this proclamation and all the other ones in this book, meditate on them and apply them in faith to your life. You can use them when you get up in the morning and before you go to sleep at night.

I believe it is more effective to actually speak them out loud rather than just read them. It is good to repeat the proclamation a number of times to enable it to sink into your spirit.

DECLARATION OF CONFIDENCE IN GOD'S PROTECTION

No weapon that is formed against me shall prosper and every tongue that arises against me in judgment I do condemn. This is my heritage as a servant of the LORD and my righteousness is from You, O LORD of Hosts.

If there are those who have been speaking or praying against me, or seeking to harm me, or who have rejected me, I forgive them (name people if you know them). Having forgiven them, I bless them in the name of the LORD.[2]

Now I declare, O LORD, that You and You alone are my God and beside You there is no other; a just God and a Savior, the Father, the Son, and the Spirit, and I worship You!

I submit myself afresh to You today in unreserved obedience. Having submitted to You, LORD, I do as Your Word directs. I resist the devil: all his pressures, his attacks, his deceptions, and every instrument or agent he would seek to use against me. I do not submit! I resist him, drive him from me and exclude him from me in the name of Jesus.

Specifically, I reject and repel infirmity, infection, pain, inflammation,

---

[2] See Matthew 5:43–45; Romans 12:14.

malignancies, allergies, viruses, _____,[3] every form of witchcraft, and every type of stress.

Finally, LORD, I thank You that through the sacrifice of Jesus on the cross, I have passed out from under the curse and entered into the blessing of Abraham whom You blessed in all things: exaltation, health, reproductiveness, prosperity, victory, God's favor, and God's friendship.[4]

                                    Amen

The following scriptural proclamations have been tested and tried in our own experience. The passages we have memorized have been taken from the particular Bible version that the Holy Spirit has made alive to us. Once again, where we have felt it appropriate to make changes in the scriptural wording, this has been indicated by an asterisk (*).

After a while, you will probably find other Scriptures that the Holy Spirit makes alive to

---

[3] Name any sicknesses or spirits that you feel have been coming against you.

[4] See Galatians 3:13–14; Genesis 24:1.

you in a special way. The blank lines at the end of each section are for you to write out these personal prayers and proclamations.

I pray that these Scriptures will do as much for you as they have done for us. They have made the difference between defeat and victory!

Chapter Sixteen

The Fear of the Lord

The fear of the Lord, that is wisdom,
And to depart from evil is understanding.

(Job 28:28)

But as for me, I trust in You, O LORD;
I say, "You are my God."
    My times are in Your hand.
Oh, how great is Your goodness,
    Which You have laid up for those who
        fear You,
Which You have prepared for us who trust
    in You
    In the presence of the sons of men!
You shall hide us in the secret place of
    Your presence
    From the plots of man;
You shall keep us secretly in a pavilion
    From the strife of tongues

(Psalm 31:14–15, 19–20)

Come, you children, listen to me;
    I will teach you the fear of the LORD.
Who is the man who desires life,
    And loves many days, that he may see
    good?
Keep your tongue from evil,
    And your lips from speaking guile.
Depart from evil, and do good; seek peace,
    and pursue it.

(Psalm 34:11–14)

The fear of the LORD is the beginning of
    wisdom;
A good understanding have all those who
    practice it.
His praise endures forever.

(Psalm 111:10*)

The fear of the LORD is the beginning of
    knowledge,
But fools despise wisdom and instruction.

(Proverbs 1:7)

The fear of the LORD is to hate evil;
Pride and arrogance and the evil way
And the perverse mouth I hate.

(Proverbs 8:13)

The fear of the LORD is the beginning of
  wisdom,
And the knowledge of the Holy One is
  understanding.
For by me your days will be multiplied,
And years of life will be added to you.

(Proverbs 9:10–11)

In the fear of the LORD there is strong
  confidence,
And His children will have a place of
  refuge.
The fear of the LORD is a fountain of life,
To avoid the snares of death.

(Proverbs 14:26–27)

The fear of the LORD leads to life,
And he who has it will abide in
  satisfaction;
He will not be visited with evil.

(Proverbs 19:23)

By humility and the fear of the LORD
Are riches and honor and life.

(Proverbs 22:4)

Personal Prayers and Proclamations

_____

_____

_____

_____

_____

_____

_____

_____

_____

_____

_____

_____

_____

_____

_____

_____

Chapter Seventeen

Righteousness and Holiness

Therefore we also, since we are surrounded by so great a cloud of witnesses, let us lay aside every weight, and the sin which so easily ensnares us, and let us run with endurance the race that is set before us,

looking unto Jesus, the author and finisher of our faith, who for the joy that was set before Him endured the cross, despising the shame, and has sat down at the right hand of the throne of God.

But we have come to Mount Zion and to the city of the living God, the heavenly Jerusalem, to an innumerable company of angels to the festal array,

to the church of the firstborn who are registered in heaven, to God the Judge of all, to the spirits of just men made perfect,

to Jesus the Mediator of the new covenant, and to the blood of sprinkling that speaks better things than that of Abel.

(Hebrews 12:1–2; 22–24*)

And this we pray, that our love may abound still more and more in knowledge and all discernment,

that we may approve the things that are excellent, that we may be sincere and without offense till the day of Christ,

being filled with the fruits of righteousness which are by Jesus Christ, to the glory and praise of God.

(Philippians 1:9–11)

Who can understand his errors?
Cleanse me from secret faults.
Keep back Your servant also from presumptuous sins;
Let them not have dominion over me.
Then I shall be blameless,
And I shall be innocent of great
  transgression.
Let the words of my mouth and the
  meditation of my heart
Be acceptable in Your sight,
O LORD, my strength and my Redeemer.

(Psalm 19:12–14)

But the hour is coming, and now is, when the true worshippers will worship the Father in spirit and truth; for the Father is seeking such to worship Him.

God is Spirit, and those who worship Him must worship in spirit and truth.

(John 4:23–24)

This is our prayer:

That we may be filled with the knowledge of His will in all wisdom and spiritual understanding;

that we may have a walk worthy of the Lord, fully pleasing Him, being fruitful in every good work and increasing in the knowledge of God;

strengthened with all might, according to His glorious power, for all patience and long suffering with joy;

giving thanks to the Father who has qualified us to be partakers of the inheritance of the saints in the light.

He has delivered us from the domain of darkness and translated us into the kingdom of the Son of His love,

in whom we have redemption through

His blood, the forgiveness of sins.

(Colossians 1:9–14*)

My son, if you receive my words,
And treasure my commands within you,
So that you incline your ear to wisdom,
And apply your heart to understanding;
Yes, if you cry out for discernment,
And lift up your voice for understanding,
If you seek her as silver,
And search for her as for hidden treasures;
Then you will understand the fear of the
   LORD,
And find the knowledge of God.

(Proverbs 2:1–5)

Now may the God of peace Himself
sanctify us completely; and may our
whole spirit, soul, and body be preserved
blameless at the coming of our Lord Jesus
Christ.

He who calls us is faithful, who also
will do it.

(1 Thessalonians 5:23–24)

Blessed is the man
Who walks not in the counsel of the ungodly,
Nor stands in the path of sinners,
Nor sits in the seat of the scornful;
But his delight is in the law of the LORD,
And in His law he meditates day and
  night.
He shall be like a tree planted by the
  rivers of water,
That brings forth its fruit in its season,
Whose leaf also shall not wither;
And whatever he does shall prosper.

(Psalm 1:1–3)

Thus says the High and Lofty One
Who inhabits eternity, whose name is Holy:
  "I dwell in the high and holy place, with
  him who has a contrite and humble
  spirit, to revive the spirit of the humble,
  and to revive the heart of the contrite
  ones.
This is the one I esteem:
  He who is humble and contrite in spirit,
  And trembles at my word."

(Isaiah 57:15; Isaiah 66:2 NIV)

As the elect of God, holy and beloved, we put on tender mercies, kindness, humbleness of mind, meekness, long suffering;

bearing with one another, and forgiving one another, if anyone has a complaint against another; even as Christ forgave us, so we also must do.

But above all these things we put on love, which is the bond of perfection.

We let the peace of God rule in our hearts, to which also we were called in one body; and we are thankful.

We let the word of Christ dwell in us richly in all wisdom, teaching and admonishing one another in psalms and hymns and spiritual songs, singing with grace in our hearts to the Lord.

And whatever we do in word or deed, we do all in the name of the Lord Jesus, giving thanks to God the Father through Him.

(Colossians 3:12–17*)

The grace of God that brings salvation has appeared to all men,

teaching us that, denying ungodliness and worldly lusts, we should live soberly, righteously, and godly in the present age,

looking for the blessed hope and glorious appearing of our great God and Savior Jesus Christ,

who gave Himself for us, that He might redeem us from every lawless deed and purify for Himself His own special people, zealous for good works.

(Titus 2:11–14)

Beloved, let us love one another, for love is of God; and everyone who loves is born of God and knows God.

He who does not love does not know God, for God is love.

In this the love of God was manifested toward us, that God has sent His only begotten Son into the world, that we might live through Him.

In this is love, not that we loved God, but that He loved us and sent His Son to be the propitiation for our sins.

Beloved, if God so loved us, we also ought to love one another.

We have known and believed the love that God has for us. God is love, and he who abides in love abides in God, and God in him.

(1 John 4:7–11, 16)

Finally, there is laid up for me
    the crown of righteousness,
    which the Lord, the righteous Judge,
    will give to me on that Day,
and not to me only
    but also to all who have loved His
    appearing.

(2 Timothy 4:8)

Blessed are the poor in spirit,
    For theirs is the kingdom of heaven.
Blessed are those who mourn,
    For they shall be comforted.
Blessed are the meek,
    For they shall inherit the earth.
Blessed are those who hunger and thirst
 for righteousness,
    For they shall be filled.
Blessed are the merciful,

For they shall obtain mercy.
Blessed are the pure in heart,
For they shall see God.
Blessed are the peacemakers,
For they shall be called sons of God.
Blessed are those who are persecuted for
righteousness' sake,
For theirs is the kingdom of heaven.

Blessed are you when they revile and
persecute you, and say all kinds of evil
against you falsely for My sake.

Rejoice and be exceedingly glad, for
great is your reward in heaven, for so they
persecuted the prophets who were before
you.

(Matthew 5:3–12)

Personal Prayers and Proclamations

_____

_____

_____

_____

_____

_____

_____

_____

_____

_____

_____

_____

_____

_____

_____

_____

Chapter Eighteen

Health and Strength

Have you not known?
Have you not heard?
The everlasting God, the LORD,
The Creator of the ends of the earth,
Neither faints nor is weary.

There is no searching of His
  understanding.

He gives power to the weak,

And to those who have no might He
  increases strength.

Even the youths shall faint and be weary,

And the young men shall utterly fall,

But those who wait on the LORD

Shall renew their strength;

They shall mount up with wings like
  eagles,

They shall run and not be weary,

They shall walk and not faint.

(Isaiah 40:28–31)

    God's strength is made perfect in my
weakness, so when I am weak, then I am
strong.

(Based on 2 Corinthians 12:9–10)

The righteous will flourish like a palm
  tree,

  they will grow like a cedar of Lebanon;

planted in the house of the LORD,

  they will flourish in the courts of our
    God.

They will still bear fruit in old age,

  they will stay fresh and green,

proclaiming, "The LORD is upright;

  He is my Rock, and there is no
    wickedness in Him."

(Psalm 92:12–15 NIV*)

But I will hope continually,

And will praise You yet more and more.

My mouth shall tell of Your righteousness

And of Your salvation all the day,

For I do not know their limits.

I will go in the strength of the Lord GOD;

I will make mention of Your righteousness,
  of Yours only.

O God, You have taught me from my youth;

And to this day I declare Your wondrous
  works.

Now also, even if I become old and
  grayheaded,

O God, do not forsake me,

Until I declare Your strength to this
  generation,
Your power to everyone who is to come.

(Psalm 71:14–18*)

My son, let them not depart from your
  eyes—
Keep sound wisdom and discretion;
So they will be life to your soul
And grace to your neck.
Then you will walk safely in your way,
And your foot will not stumble.
When you lie down, you will not be afraid;
Yes, you will lie down and your sleep will
  be sweet.
Do not be afraid of sudden terror,
Nor of trouble from the wicked when it
  comes;
For the LORD will be your confidence,
And will keep your foot from being caught.

(Proverbs 3:21–26)

I can do all things through the One who
empowers me within.[5]

(Philippians 4:13)

---

[5] Direct translation from the original Greek.

The LORD will give strength to His people;
The LORD will bless His people with peace.

(Psalm 29:11)

O God, You are more awesome than Your
  holy places.
The God of Israel is He who gives strength
  and power to His people.
Blessed be God!   *(Psalm 68:35)*

My son, attend to my words;
    incline thine ear unto my sayings.
Let them not depart from thine eyes;
    keep them in the midst of thine heart.
For they are life unto those that find them,
    and health to all their flesh.
Keep thy heart with all diligence;
    for out of it are the issues of life.

(Proverbs 4:20–23 KJV)

Now the Lord is the Spirit;
   and where the Spirit of the Lord is,
      there is liberty.
But we all, with unveiled face,
   beholding as in a mirror the glory of the
   Lord, are being transformed into the
   same image from
      glory to glory,
   just as by the Spirit of the Lord.

(2 Corinthians 3:17–18)

Personal Prayers and Proclamations

_____

_____

_____

_____

_____

_____

_____

_____

_____

_____

_____

_____

_____

_____

_____

Guidance, Protection, and Preservation

The LORD shall preserve me from all evil;
He shall preserve my soul.
The LORD shall preserve my going out and
my coming in
From this time forth, and even
forevermore.

There is a path which no fowl knoweth,
and which the vulture's eye hath not
seen:
The lion's whelps have not trodden it,
nor the fierce lion passed by it....
Seeing it is hid from the eyes of all living,
and kept close from the fowls of the air.
(Psalm 121:7–8; Job 28:7–8, 21 KJV)

The LORD is my light and my salvation;
Whom shall I fear?
The LORD is the strength of my life;
Of whom shall I be afraid?
When the wicked came against me

To eat up my flesh,
My enemies and foes,
They stumbled and fell.
Though an army may encamp against me,
My heart shall not fear;
Though war should rise against me,
In this I will be confident.
One thing I have desired of the LORD,
That will I seek:
That I may dwell in the house of the LORD
All the days of my life,
To behold the beauty of the LORD,
And to inquire in His temple.
For in the time of trouble
He shall hide me in His pavilion;
In the secret place of His tabernacle
He shall hide me;
He shall set me high upon a rock.
And now my head shall be lifted up above
  my enemies all around me;
Therefore I will offer sacrifices of joy in His
  tabernacle;
I will sing, yes, I will sing praises to the
  LORD.

(Psalm 27:1–6)

See, I am sending an angel ahead of you to guard you along the way and to bring you to the place I have prepared.

Pay attention to him and listen to what he says. Do not rebel against him; he will not forgive your rebellion, since My Name is in him.

If you listen carefully to what he says and do all that I say, I will be an enemy to your enemies and will oppose those who oppose you.

My angel will go ahead of you and bring you into the land of the Amorites, Hittites, Perizzites, Canaanites, Hivites and Jebusites, and I will wipe them out.

Do not bow down before their gods or worship them or follow their practices. You must demolish them and break their sacred stones to pieces.

Worship the LORD your God, and His blessing will be on your food and water.

I will take away sickness from among you, and none will miscarry or be barren in your land. I will give you a full life span.

I will send my terror ahead of you and throw into confusion every nation you encounter.

I will make all your enemies turn their backs and run.

(Exodus 23:20–27 NIV)

I shall not die, but live,
And declare the works of the LORD.

(Psalm 118:17)

Unless the LORD builds the house,
They labor in vain who build it;
Unless the LORD guards the city,
The watchman stays awake in vain.

(Psalm 127:1)

I trust in the LORD with all my heart,
    And do not lean on my own
        understanding;
In all my ways I acknowledge Him,
    And He directs my paths.
I am not wise in my own eyes;
    I fear the LORD and depart from evil.
It will be health to my inward parts,
    And strength to my bones.

(Proverbs 3:5–8)

This Book of the Law shall not depart from your mouth, but you shall meditate in it day and night, that you may observe to do according to all that is written in it. For then you will make your way prosperous, and then you will have good success.

Have I not commanded you? Be strong and of good courage; do not be afraid, nor be dismayed, for the LORD your God is with you wherever you go.

(Joshua 1:8–9)

The LORD is good,
A stronghold in the day of trouble;
And He knows those who trust in Him.

(Nahum 1:7)

Blessed is the man whom You instruct,
  O LORD,
    And teach out of Your law,
That You may give him relief from the days
  of adversity,
    Until the pit is dug for the wicked.

(Psalm 94:12–13)

Fear not, for I am with you;
    Be not dismayed, for I am your God.
I will strengthen you,
Yes, I will help you,
I will uphold you with the right hand of My
  righteousness.

(Isaiah 41:10*)

I know the plans I have for you.
    Plans of peace and not of evil,
    Plans of prosperity and not of calamity,
    To give you hope and a future.

(Jeremiah 29:11 NIV*)

As for God, His way is perfect;
The word of the LORD is proven;
He is a shield to all who trust in Him.

(Psalm 18:30)

The Lord will deliver me from every evil
  work
And preserve me for His heavenly
  kingdom.
To Him be glory forever and ever. Amen!

(2 Timothy 4:18)

You pushed me violently, that I might fall,
But the LORD helped me.
The LORD is my strength and my song,
And He has become my salvation.
The voice of rejoicing and salvation
Is in the tents of the righteous;
The right hand of the LORD does valiantly.
The right hand of the LORD is exalted;
The right hand of the LORD does
valiantly.
I shall not die, but live,
And declare the works of the LORD.
The LORD has chastened me severely,
But He has not given me over to death.

(Psalm 118:13–18)

Through the Lord's mercies we are not
consumed,
Because His compassions fail not.
They are new every morning;
Great is Your faithfulness.
"The LORD is my portion," says my soul,
"Therefore I hope in Him!"
The LORD is good to those who wait for
Him,

To the soul who seeks Him.

It is good that one should hope and wait quietly

For the salvation of the LORD.

(Lamentations 3:22–26)

Let all those rejoice who put their trust in You;

Let them ever shout for joy,

because You protect and defend them;

Let those also who love Your name

Be joyful in You.

For You, O LORD, will bless the righteous;

With favor You will surround him as with a shield.

(Psalm 5:11–12)

Personal Prayers and Proclamations

_____

_____

_____

_____

_____

_____

_____

_____

_____

_____

_____

_____

_____

_____

_____

_____

Chapter Twenty

God's Intervention in Human Affairs

Blessed be the name of God forever and
ever,
For wisdom and might are His.
And He changes the times and the seasons;
He removes kings and raises up kings;
He gives wisdom to the wise
And knowledge to those who have
understanding.
He reveals deep and secret things;
He knows what is in the darkness,
And the light dwells with Him....

For His dominion is an everlasting
dominion,
And His kingdom is from generation to
generation.
All the inhabitants of the earth are
reputed as nothing;
He does according to His will in the army
of heaven
And among the inhabitants of the earth.

No one can restrain His hand
Or say to Him, "What have You done?"
(Daniel 2:20–22; 4:34–35)

For by grace we have been saved through faith, and that not of ourselves; it is the gift of God, not of works, lest anyone should boast.

For we are His workmanship, created in Christ Jesus for good works, which God prepared beforehand that we should walk in them.

(Ephesians 2:8–10)

Show Your marvelous loving kindness by
 Your right hand,
O You who save those who trust in You
From those who rise up against them.
Keep me as the apple of Your eye;
Hide me in the shadow of Your wings,
From the wicked who oppress me,
From my deadly enemies who surround
 me.

(Psalm 17:7–9)

LORD, there is no one like you to help the powerless against the mighty. Help us, O LORD our God, for we rely on you, and in your name we have come against this vast army. O LORD, you are our God; do not let man prevail against you.

(2 Chronicles 14:11 NIV)

O LORD, God of our fathers, are You not the God who is in heaven?
You rule over all the kingdoms of the nations.
Power and might are in Your hand, and no one can withstand You.

(2 Chronicles 20:6 NIV)

We remember the prisoners as if chained with them;
   and those who are mistreated;
   since we ourselves are in the body also.

(Hebrews 13:3)

And to the angel of the church in Philadelphia write,
"These things says He who is holy, He who is true,
He who has the key of David,
He who opens and no one shuts,

and shuts and no one opens:

> 'I know your works.
> See, I have set before you an open door,
> and no one can shut it;
> for you have a little strength,
> have kept My word,
> and have not denied My name.'"

(Revelation 3:7–8)

Let them all be confounded and turned
  back that hate Zion.
Let them be as the grass on the housetops,
   which withers before it grows up.

(Psalm 129:5–6)

Destroy, O Lord, and divide their
  tongues....

(Psalm 55:9)

The scepter of the wicked will not remain over the land allotted to the righteous.

(Psalm 125:3 NIV)

Seek the LORD,
   all you meek of the earth,
   Who have upheld His justice.

Seek righteousness, seek humility.
It may be that you will be hidden
   In the day of the LORD's anger.

               (Zephaniah 2:3)

For the LORD will not forsake His people,
   for His great name's sake,
Because it has pleased the LORD
   to make Israel His people.

             (1 Samuel 12:22*)

   Remember Abraham, Isaac, and Israel,
Your servants, to whom You swore by Your
own self, and said to them, "I will multiply
your descendants as the stars of heaven;
and all this land that I have spoken of I
give to your descendants, and they shall
inherit it forever."

               (Exodus 32:13)

Let all the earth fear the LORD;
Let all the inhabitants of the world stand
  in awe of Him.
For He spoke, and it was done;
He commanded, and it stood fast.
The LORD brings the counsel of the nations
  to nothing;

He makes the plans of the peoples of no
   effect.

The counsel of the Lord stands forever,

The plans of His heart to all generations.

Blessed is the nation whose God is the
   Lord,

And the people He has chosen as His own
   inheritance.

(Psalm 33:8–12)

"If it had not been the Lord who was on
our side,"

   Let Israel now say—

"If it had not been the Lord who was on
our side,

When men rose up against us,

Then they would have swallowed us alive,

When their wrath was kindled against us;

   Then the waters would have
     overwhelmed us,

   The stream would have gone swept our
     soul;

   Then the swollen waters would have
     swept over our soul."

Blessed be the Lord,

   Who has not given us as prey to their
     teeth.

Our soul has escaped as a bird from the
  snare of the fowlers;
The snare is broken, and we have escaped.
Our help is in the name of the LORD,
    Who made heaven and earth.

(Psalm 124)

Pray for the peace of Jerusalem:
    "May they prosper who love you.
Peace be within your walls,
    prosperity within your palaces."

(Psalm 122:6–7)

Personal Prayers and Proclamations

_____

_____

_____

_____

_____

_____

_____

_____

_____

_____

_____

_____

_____

_____

_____

Chapter Twenty-one

Testing and Trials

But thanks be to God, who gives us the victory through our Lord Jesus Christ.

Therefore, my beloved brethren, be steadfast, immovable, always abounding in the work of the Lord, knowing that your labor is not in vain in the Lord.

(1 Corinthians 15:57–58)

I will bless the LORD at all times;
    His praise shall continually be in my
      mouth.
My soul shall make its boast in the LORD;
    The humble shall hear of it and be glad.
Oh, magnify the LORD with me,
    And let us exalt His name together.
I sought the LORD, and He heard me,
    And delivered me from all my fears.

(Psalm 34:1–4)

Therefore we submit to God.
We resist the devil and he will flee from us.

(James 4:7)

Therefore I endure all things for the sake of the elect, that they also may obtain the salvation which is in Christ Jesus with eternal glory.

This is a faithful saying:
For if we died with Him,
  We shall also live with Him.
If we endure,
  We shall also reign with Him.
If we deny Him,
  He also will deny us.
If we are faithless,
  He remains faithful;
He cannot deny Himself.

(2 Timothy 2:10–13)

We count it all joy when we fall into
  various trials,
    knowing that the testing of our faith
    produces endurance.
But we let endurance have its perfect work,
    that we may be perfect and complete,
    lacking nothing.

(James 1:2–4*)

Blessed be the God and Father of our Lord Jesus Christ, who according to His abundant mercy has begotten us again to a living hope through the resurrection of Jesus Christ from the dead,

to an inheritance incorruptible and undefiled and that does not fade away, reserved in heaven for us,

who are kept by the power of God through faith for salvation ready to be revealed in the last time.

In this we greatly rejoice, though now for a little while, if need be, we have been distressed by various trials,

that the genuineness of our faith, being much more precious than gold that perishes, though it is tested by fire, may be found to praise, honor, and glory at the revelation of Jesus Christ, whom having not seen we love.

Though now we do not see Him, yet believing, we rejoice with joy inexpressible and full of glory,

receiving the end of our faith; the salvation of our souls.

(1 Peter 1:3–9)

Blessed is the man who trusts in the LORD,
  And whose hope is in the LORD.
For he shall be like a tree planted by the
  waters,
  Which spreads out its roots by the river,
And will not fear when heat comes;
  But its leaf will be green,
And will not be anxious in the year of
  drought,
  Nor will cease from yielding fruit.
                      (Jeremiah 17:7–8)

If God is for us, who can be against us?
He who did not spare His own Son, but
delivered Him up for us all, how shall He
not with Him also freely give us all things?
Who shall bring a charge against God's
elect? It is God who justifies. Who is he
who condemns? It is Christ who died, and
furthermore is also risen, who is even at
the right hand of God, who also makes in-
tercession for us.
Who shall separate us from the love of
Christ?
      Shall tribulation, or distress,
      Or persecution, or famine,

Or nakedness, or peril, or sword?
As it is written:

"For Your sake we are killed all day
long;
We are accounted as sheep for the
slaughter."

Yet in all these things we are more
than conquerors through
Him who loved us.

For I am persuaded that neither death
nor life,
Nor angels nor principalities nor
powers,
Nor things present nor things to
come,
Nor height nor depth, nor any other

created thing, shall be able to separate
us from the love of God which is in Christ
Jesus our Lord.

(Romans 8:31–39)

Personal Prayers and Proclamations

_____

_____

_____

_____

_____

_____

_____

_____

_____

_____

_____

_____

_____

_____

_____

_____

Chapter Twenty-two

Spiritual Conflict

God resists the proud,
But gives grace to the humble.

Therefore we humble ourselves under the mighty hand of God, that He may exalt us in due time,

having cast all our care upon Him, for He cares for us.

We are sober, we are vigilant; because our adversary the devil walks about like a roaring lion, seeking whom he may devour.

We resist him, steadfast in the faith, knowing that the same sufferings are experienced by our brotherhood in the world.

But the God of all grace, who called us to His eternal glory by Christ Jesus, after we have suffered a while, will perfect, establish, strengthen, and settle us.

To Him be the glory and the dominion forever and ever. Amen.

(1 Peter 5:5–11*)

For though we walk in the flesh, we do not war after the flesh:

for the weapons of our warfare are not carnal, but mighty through God to the pulling down of strongholds;

casting down imaginations, and every high thing that exalteth itself against the knowledge of God, and bringing into captivity every thought to the obedience of Christ.

(2 Corinthians 10:3–5 KJV)

We overcome Satan by the blood of the Lamb
and by the word of our testimony,
and we do not love our lives to the death.

(Revelation 12:11)

The bolts of our gates will be iron and bronze,
and your strength will equal our days.
There is no one like the God of Jeshurun,
who rides on the heavens to help us
and on the clouds in his majesty.
The eternal God is our refuge,
and underneath are the everlasting arms.

He will drive out our enemy before us,
saying, "Destroy him!"
(Deuteronomy 33:25–27 NIV)

No weapon that is formed against us
shall prosper; and every tongue which rises
against us in judgment we do condemn.
This is our heritage as servants of the
LORD, and our righteousness is from You, O
LORD of hosts.
(Isaiah 54:17 KJV*)

Plead my cause, O LORD,
with those who strive against me;
Fight against those who fight against me.
Take hold of shield and buckler,
And stand up for my help.
Also draw out the spear,
And stop the way against those who
pursue me.
Say to my soul,
"I am your salvation."
(Psalm 35:1–3*)

Personal Prayers and Proclamations

_____
_____
_____
_____
_____
_____
_____
_____
_____
_____
_____
_____
_____
_____
_____
_____

Chapter Twenty-three

Perfect Redemption

Now unto Him who is able to keep us from falling, and to present us faultless before the presence of His glory with exceeding joy,

To the only wise God our Savior, be glory and majesty, dominion and power, both now and forever. Amen.

(Jude 24–25 KJV)

Bless the LORD, O my soul: and all that is within me, bless His holy name.

Bless the LORD, O my soul, and forget not all His benefits:

Who forgiveth all thine iniquities; who healeth all thy diseases;

Who redeemeth thy life from destruction; who crowneth thee with lovingkindness and tender mercies;

Who satisfieth thy mouth with good things; so that thy youth is renewed like the eagle's.

(Psalm 103:1–5 KJV)

This is our prayer:

that the God of our Lord Jesus Christ, the Father of glory, may give to us a spirit of wisdom and revelation in the knowledge of Him,

the eyes of our understanding being enlightened; that we may know what is the hope of His calling, what are the riches of the glory of His inheritance in the saints,

and what is the exceeding greatness of His power toward us who believe, according to the working of His mighty power which He worked in Christ when He raised Him from the dead and seated Him at His right hand in the heavenly places,

far above all principality and power and might and dominion, and every name that is named, not only in this age but also in that which is to come.

And He put all things under His feet, and gave Him to be head over all things to the church,

which is His body, the fullness of Him who fills all in all.

(Ephesians 1:17–23)

We are confident of this very thing, that He who has begun a good work in us will complete it until the day of Jesus Christ.

(Philippians 1:6)

For by one sacrifice He has perfected forever us who are being sanctified.

(Hebrews 10:14*)

There is therefore now no condemnation to those who are in Christ Jesus....

For the law of the Spirit of life in Christ Jesus has made me free from the law of sin and death.

(Romans 8:1–2)

Through the sacrifice of Jesus on the cross, I have passed out from under the curse and entered into the blessing of Abraham, whom God blessed in all things.

(Based on Galatians 3:13–14; Genesis 24:1)

Behold what manner of love the Father has bestowed on us, that we should be called children of God! And we are.

Therefore the world does not know us, because it did not know Him.

Beloved, now we are children of God;

and it has not yet been revealed what we shall be,

but we know that when He is revealed,

we shall be like Him, for we shall see Him as He is.

And everyone who has this hope in Him purifies himself, just as He is pure.

(1 John 3:1–3)

We have known and believed the love
    that God has for us.
God is love, and he who abides in love
    abides in God, and God in him.

(1 John 4:16)

But we are washed, but we are sanctified,
but we are justified in the name of the
    Lord Jesus
and by the Spirit of our God.

(1 Corinthians 6:11)

Now may the God of peace who brought up our Lord Jesus from the dead, that great Shepherd of the sheep, through the blood of the everlasting covenant,

make us perfect in every good work to do His will,

working in us what is well pleasing in His sight, through Jesus Christ,

to whom be glory forever and ever. Amen.

(Hebrews 13:20–21)

Personal Prayers and Proclamations

_____

_____

_____

_____

_____

_____

_____

_____

_____

_____

_____

_____

_____

_____

_____

_____

Chapter Twenty-four

Mental and Emotional Stability

We have labored and been heavy laden, but we come to You, Lord Jesus, that You may give us rest.

We take Your yoke upon us and learn from You, for You are meek and lowly in heart, and we shall find rest for our souls.

For Your yoke is easy and Your burden is light.

(Matthew 11:28–30*)

There remains therefore a Sabbath-rest for the people of God.

For he who has entered His rest has himself also ceased from his works as God did from His.

Let us therefore be diligent to enter that rest, lest anyone fall according to the same example of disobedience.

(Hebrews 4:9–11*)

You will keep me in perfect peace, because my mind is stayed on You and I trust in You.

(Isaiah 26:3*)

I have great peace because I love Your law and nothing shall offend me.

(Psalm 119:165 KJV*)

The weapons of my warfare are mighty in God.

With them I pull down strongholds that Satan has built in my mind.

I bring all my thoughts into obedience to Christ.

Three of my mightiest weapons are proclamation,

thanksgiving, and praise.

(Based on 2 Corinthians 10:4–5)

God has not given me a spirit of fear,

but of power and of love and of a sound mind.

(2 Timothy 1:7)

Now may the God of hope fill us with all joy and peace in believing, that we may abound in hope by the power of the Holy Spirit.

(Romans 15:13)

We are anxious for nothing, but in everything by prayer and supplication, with thanksgiving, we let our requests be made known to God;

and the peace of God, which surpasses all understanding, will guard our hearts and minds in Christ Jesus.

Finally, brethren,

whatever things are true,

whatever things are noble,

whatever things are just,

whatever things are pure,

whatever things are lovely,

whatever things are of good report,

if there is any virtue

and if there is anything praiseworthy;

we meditate on these things.

(Philippians 4:6–8)

Personal Prayers and Proclamations

_____

_____

_____

_____

_____

_____

_____

_____

_____

_____

_____

_____

_____

_____

_____

_____

Chapter Twenty-five

Serving God

But thanks be to God, who always leads us in triumphal procession in Christ and through us spreads everywhere the fragrance of the knowledge of Him.

For we are to God the aroma of Christ among those who are being saved and those who are perishing.

To the one we are the smell of death; to the other, the fragrance of life. And who is equal to such a task?

Unlike so many, we do not peddle the word of God for profit. On the contrary, in Christ we speak before God with sincerity, like men sent from God.

(2 Corinthians 2:14–17 NIV)

God is able to do exceedingly abundantly
    above all that we ask or think,
        according to the power that works in us.
(Ephesians 3:20*)

God is able to make all grace abound toward us; that we, always having all sufficiency in all things, may abound to every good work.

(2 Corinthians 9:8 KJV)

Again I say to you that if two of you agree on earth concerning anything that they ask, it will be done for them by My Father in heaven.

(Matthew 18:19)

The harvest truly is plenteous, but the laborers are few;
Therefore we pray the Lord of the harvest, that He will thrust forth laborers into His harvest.

(Matthew 9:37–38 KJV*)

And this gospel of the kingdom will be proclaimed in all the world as a witness to all the nations, and then the end will come.

(Matthew 24:14*)

We will be strong and of good courage, and
do it;

> we will not fear nor be dismayed,
>
> for the LORD God—our God—will be
> with us.

He will not leave us nor forsake us,

> until we have finished all the work
>
> for the service of the house of the LORD.

(1 Chronicles 28:20)

For as the rain comes down, and the snow
from heaven,

> And do not return there,

But water the earth,

> And make it bring forth and bud,

That it may give seed to the sower

> And bread to the eater,

So shall My word be that goes forth from
My mouth;

> It shall not return to Me void,

But it shall accomplish what I please,

> And it shall prosper in the thing for
> which I sent it.

(Isaiah 55:10–11)

We work out our own salvation with fear
 and trembling;

> for it is God who works in us both to will
>
> and to do for His good pleasure.

We do all things without grumbling and
 arguing,

> that we may become blameless and
> innocent,
>
> children of God without fault
>
> in the midst of a crooked and perverse
> generation,
>
> among whom we shine as lights in the
> world,
>
> holding forth the word of life.
>
> > *(Philippians 2:12–16*)*

Let us watch, stand fast in the faith,

> be brave, be strong.

Let all that we do be done with love.

> > *(1 Corinthians 16:13–14)*

What things were gain to me, these I
have counted loss for Christ.

But indeed I also count all things loss
for the excellence of the knowledge of
Christ Jesus my Lord, for whom I have suffered the loss of all things, and count them

as rubbish, that I may gain Christ

and be found in Him, not having my own righteousness, which is from the law, but that which is through faith in Christ, the righteousness which is from God by faith;

that I may know Him and the power of His resurrection, and the fellowship of His sufferings, being conformed to His death,

if, by any means, I may attain to the resurrection from the dead.

Not that I have already attained, or am already perfected; but I press on, that I may lay hold of that for which Christ Jesus has also laid hold of me.

Brethren, I do not count myself to have apprehended; but one thing I do, forgetting those things which are behind and reaching forward to those things which are ahead,

I press toward the goal for the prize of the upward call of God in Christ Jesus.

(Philippians 3:7–14)

But you, O man of God, flee these things

> and pursue righteousness, godliness,
>
> faith, love, patience, gentleness.

Fight the good fight of faith, lay hold on eternal life,

to which you were also called and have confessed the good

confession in the presence of many witnesses.

> I urge you in the sight of God who gives life to all things,
>
> and before Christ Jesus who witnessed the good confession

before Pontius Pilate,

> that you keep this command without spot,
>
> blameless until our Lord Jesus Christ's appearing,
>
> which He will manifest in His own time,

He who is the blessed and only Potentate,

> the King of kings and Lord of lords,
>
> who alone has immortality,
>
> dwelling in unapproachable light,
>
> whom no man has seen or can see,
>
> to Whom be honor and everlasting power. Amen.

(1 Timothy 6:11–16)

"Now the just shall live by faith;
But if anyone draws back,
My soul has no pleasure in him."
But we are not of those who draw back to
  perdition,
    but of those who believe to the saving of
    the soul.

(Hebrews 10:38–39*)

If then we were raised with Christ,
    we seek those things which are above,
    where Christ is, sitting at the right
    hand of God.
We set our minds on things above,
    not on things on the earth.
For we died, and our lives are hidden
    with Christ in God.
When Christ who is our life appears,
    then we also will appear with Him in
    glory.

(Colossians 3:1–4)

I have been crucified with Christ;
>it is no longer I who live, but Christ
>>lives in me;
and the life which I now live in the flesh
>I live by faith in the Son of God,
>Who loved me
>and gave Himself for me.

>>>>*(Galatians 2:20*)*

Personal Prayers and Proclamations

_____
_____
_____
_____
_____
_____
_____
_____
_____
_____
_____
_____
_____
_____
_____
_____
_____

Chapter Twenty-six

The Divine Exchange

Jesus was **punished**
that we might be **forgiven**.[6]
Jesus was **wounded**
that we might be **healed**.[7]
Jesus was made **sin with our sinfulness**
that we might be
made **righteous with His righteousness**.[8]
Jesus died our **death**
that we might receive His **life**.[9]
Jesus was made a **curse**
that we might enter into the **blessing**.[10]
Jesus endured our **poverty**
that we might share His **abundance**.[11]
Jesus bore our **shame**
that we might share His **glory**.[12]

---

[6] See Isaiah 53:4–5.
[7] Ibid.
[8] See Isaiah 53:10; 2 Corinthians 5:21.
[9] See Hebrews 2:9.
[10] See Galatians 3:13–14.
[11] See 2 Corinthians 8:9, 9:8.
[12] See Matthew 27:35–36; Hebrews 12:2; 2:9.

Jesus endured our **rejection**

> that we might have His **acceptance**
> with the Father.[13]

Jesus was **cut off** by death

> that we might be **joined** to God
> eternally.[14]

Our **old man** was put to death in Him

> that the **new man** might come to life
> in us.[15]

---

[13] See Matthew 27:46–51; Ephesians 1:5–6.

[14] See Isaiah 53:8; 1 Corinthians 6:17.

[15] See Romans 6:6; Colossians 3:9–10.

Chapter Twenty-seven

Confession for Overcomers
(Let the Redeemed Say So)[16]

My body is a temple for the Holy Spirit[17], redeemed[18], cleansed[19], and sanctified by the blood of Jesus.[20]

My members, the parts of my body, are instruments of righteousness[21], yielded to God for His service and for His glory.

The devil has no place in me, no power over me, no unsettled claims against me.

All has been settled by the blood of Jesus.[22]

I overcome Satan by the blood of the Lamb and by the word of my testimony, and I do not love my life to the death.[23]

---

[16] See Psalm 107:2.
[17] See 1 Corinthians 6:19.
[18] See Ephesians 1:7.
[19] See 1 John 1:7.
[20] See Hebrews 13:12.
[21] See Romans 6:13.
[22] See Romans 3:23–25, 8:33–34.
[23] See Revelation 12:11.

My body is for the Lord and the Lord is for my body.[24]

Chapter Twenty-eight

By This I Overcome the Devil

We overcome Satan when we testify personally to what the Word of God says the blood of Jesus does for us.[25]

Through the blood of Jesus,

> I am redeemed out of the hand of the devil.[26]

Through the blood of Jesus, all my sins are forgiven.[27]

Through the blood of Jesus,

> I am continually being cleansed from all sin.[28]

Through the blood of Jesus,

> I am justified, made righteous, just-as-if-I'd never sinned.[29]

Through the blood of Jesus,

> I am sanctified, made holy, set apart to God.[30]

[25] See Revelation 12:11.
[26] See Ephesians 1:7.
[27] See 1 John 1:9.
[28] See 1 John 1:7.
[29] See Romans 5:9.
[30] See Hebrews 13:12.

Through the blood of Jesus,
> I have boldness to enter into the
> presence of God.[31]

The blood of Jesus cries out continually
> to God in heaven on my behalf.[32]

---

[31] See Hebrews 10:19.
[32] See Hebrews 12:24.

Chapter Twenty-nine

Declaration of Confidence in God's Protection

No weapon that is formed against me shall prosper, and every tongue that arises against me in judgment I do condemn. This is my heritage as a servant of the Lord, and my righteousness is from You, O Lord of Hosts.

If there are those who have been speaking or praying against me—or seeking to harm me, or who have rejected me—I forgive them (*name people if you know them*). Having forgiven them, I bless them in the name of the Lord.[33]

Now I declare, O Lord, that You and You alone are my God and beside You there is no other; a just God and a Savior, the Father, the Son, and the Spirit, and

---

[33] See Matthew 5:43–45; Romans 12:14.

I worship You! I submit myself afresh to You today in unreserved obedience.

Having submitted to You, Lord, I do as Your Word directs. I resist the devil: all his pressures, his attacks, his deceptions, and every instrument or agent he would seek to use against me. I do not submit! I resist him, drive him from me, and exclude him from me in Jesus' name.

Specifically, I reject and repel: infirmity, infection, pain, inflammation, malignancies, allergies, viruses, every form of witchcraft, and every type of stress (*name any specific sickness or demonic affliction that you feel has been coming against you*).

Finally, Lord, I thank You that through the sacrifice of Jesus on the cross, I have passed out from under the curse and entered into the blessings of Abraham, whom You blessed in all things: exaltation, health, reproductiveness, prosperity, victory, God's favor, and God's friendship.[34] Amen.

---

[34] See Galatians 3:13–14; Genesis 24:1.

Chapter Thirty

Proclamations on Behalf of Israel

He who scattered Israel is gathering him,
and will keep him as a shepherd keeps his
   flock.[35]

(Jeremiah 31:10)

Let them all be confounded and turned
   back that hate Zion.
Let them be as the grass upon the
   housetops,
      which withers before it grows up.
(Psalm 129:5–6 KJV)

Destroy, O LORD, and divide their tongues!
(Psalm 55:9)

The scepter of the wicked will not remain
over the land allotted to the righteous...
(Psalm 125:3 NIV)

---

[35] Changed to present tense because it is happening now.

For the LORD will not forsake his people,
  for His great name's sake,
because it has pleased the LORD
  to make Israel His people.

  (1 Samuel 12:22)

Let all the earth fear the LORD;
  Let all the inhabitants of the world
    stand in awe of Him.
For He spoke, and it was done.
  He commanded, and it stood fast.
The LORD brings the counsel of the nations
  to nothing;
    He makes the plans of the peoples of no
      effect.
The counsel of the LORD stands forever,
  The plans of His heart to all generations.
Blessed is the nation whose God is the LORD,
  The people He has chosen as His own
    inheritance.

  (Psalm 33:8–12)

Show Your marvelous lovingkindness by
Your right hand,

O You who save those who trust in You
From those who rise up against them.

Keep Israel[36] as the apple of Your eye;

Hide them under the shadow of Your
wings,

From the wicked who oppress them,

From their deadly enemies who
surround them.

(Psalm 17:7–9)

"If it had not been the LORD who was on
our side,"

Let Israel now say—

"If it had not been the LORD who was on
our side,

When men rose up against us,

Then they would have swallowed us alive,

When their wrath was kindled against
us;

Then the waters would have overwhelmed
us,

The stream would have swept over our
soul;

Then the swollen waters

Would have swept over our soul."

[36] Changed *"me"* to *"Israel"*.

Blessed be the LORD,
>   Who has not given us as prey to their
>   teeth.

Our soul has escaped as a bird from the
snare of the fowlers;
>   The snare is broken, and we have
>   escaped.

Our help is in the name of the Lord,
>   Who made heaven and earth.

(Psalm 124)

Chapter Thirty-one

Twelve Steps to a Good Year

Let us fear lest we fail to rest in Christ.

(Hebrews 4:1)

Let us be diligent.

(Hebrews 4:11)

Let us hold fast our confession.

(Hebrews 4:14)

Let us draw near to the throne of grace.

(Hebrews 4:16)

Let us press on to maturity.

(Hebrews 6:1)

Let us draw near to the Most Holy Place.

(Hebrews 10:19, 22)

Let us hold fast our confession without wavering.

(Hebrews 10:23)

Let us consider one another.

(Hebrews 10:24)

Let us run with endurance the race.

(Hebrews 12:1)

Let us show gratitude.

(Hebrews 12:28)

Let us go out to Him outside the camp.

(Hebrews 13:13)

Let us continually offer up a sacrifice of praise.

(Hebrews 13:15)

Therefore, let us fear lest, while a promise remains of entering His rest, any one of you should seem to have come short of it.

(Hebrews 4:1 NASB)

Let us therefore be diligent to enter that rest, lest anyone fall through following the same example of disobedience.

(Hebrews 4:11 NASB)

Since then we have a great high priest who has passed through the heavens, Jesus the Son of God, let us hold fast our confession.

(Hebrews 4:14 NASB)

Let us therefore draw near with confidence to the throne of grace, that we may receive mercy and may find grace to help in time of need.

(Hebrews 4:16 NASB)

Therefore leaving the elementary teaching about the Christ, let us press on to maturity.

(Hebrews 6:1 NASB)

Therefore, brothers, since we have confidence to enter the Most Holy Place by the blood of Jesus...let us draw near to God with a sincere heart.

(Hebrews 10:19, 22 NIV)

Let us hold fast the confession of our hope without wavering, for He who promised is faithful.

(Hebrews 10:23 NASB)

Let us consider how to stimulate one another to love and good deeds.

(Hebrews 10:24 NASB)

Therefore, since we have so great a cloud of witnesses surrounding us, let us also lay aside every encumbrance, and the sin which so easily entangles us, and let us run with endurance the race that is set before us.

(Hebrews 12:1 NASB)

Therefore, since we receive a kingdom which cannot be shaken, let us show gratitude, by which we may offer to God an acceptable service with reverence and awe.

(Hebrews 12:28 NASB)

Jesus also, that He might sanctify the people through His own blood, suffered outside the gate. Hence, let us go out to Him outside the camp, bearing His reproach.

(Hebrews 13:12–13 NASB)

Through Him then, let us continually offer up a sacrifice of praise to God.

(Hebrews 13:15 NASB)

SCRIPTURE INDEX

Old Testament

Genesis
24:1 .... 70, 135, 164

Exodus
23:20–27 101–102
32:13 113

Deuteronomy
33:25–27 .. 48, 128–129

Joshua
1:8–9 103

1 Samuel
12:22 .... 113, 166

1 Chronicles
28:20 149

2 Chronicles
14:11 .... 57, 111
20:6 .... 57, 111

Job
28:7–8, 21 99
28:28 73

Psalms
1:1–3 83
5:11–12 106
17:7–9 .... 110, 167
18:30 104
19:12–14 80
27:1–6 99–100
29:11 94
31:14–15, 19–20 73
33:8–12 .... 57, 114, 166
34:1–4 119
34:11–14 74
35:1–3 129
55:9 .... 112, 165
68:35 94
71:14–18 92–93
92:12–15 92
94:12–13 103
103:1–5 133
107:2 159
111:10 74
118:13–18 105
118:17 .... 45, 102
119:165 142
121:7–8 99
122:6–7 115
124 .. 114–115, 167–168
125:3 .... 61, 112, 165

127:1 102
129:5–6 .... 61, 112, 165
149:5–9 37–38

Proverbs
1:7 74
2:1–5 82
3:5–8 102
3:21–26 93
4:20–23 94
8:13 74
9:10–11 75
14:26–27 75
19:23 75
22:4 75

Isaiah
26:3 142
40:28–31 91
41:10 104
53:4–5 157
53:8 158
53:10 157
54:17 .... 47, 129
55:10–11 .... 10, 30, 149
57:15; 66:2 83
66:1–2 .... 33, 83

Jeremiah
17:7–8 122
29:11 .... 44, 104
31:7, 10 .... 62, 165

Lamentations
3:22–26 105–106

Daniel
2:20–22; 4:34–35 ....
55–56, 109–110

Nahum
1:7 103

Zephaniah
2:3 112–113

New Testament

Matthew
5:3–12.................. 86–87
5:43–45............. 69, 163
9:37–38..................... 148
11:28–30................. 141
18:19......................... 148
24:14.......... 15–16, 148
27:35–36................. 157
27:46–51................. 158

John
4:23–24..................... 81

Romans
3:23–25.................. 159
5:9............................. 161
6:6............................ 158
6:13.......................... 159
8:1–2........................ 135
8:31–39.......... 122–123
12:14................. 69, 163
15:13....................... 143

1 Corinthians
6:11.......................... 136
6:13.......................... 160
6:17.......................... 158
6:19.......................... 159
15:57–58................. 119
16:13–14................. 150

2 Corinthians
2:14–17................... 147
3:17–18..................... 95
5:21.......................... 157
8:9............................ 157
9:8............. 51, 148, 157
10:3–5............. 128, 142
12:9–10..................... 91

Galatians
2:20.......................... 153
3:13–14............ 70, 135,
                     157, 164

Ephesians
1:5–6........................ 158
1:7.................. 159, 161
1:17–23................... 134
2:8–10..................... 110
3:20.......................... 147

Philippians
1:6	135
1:9–11	80
2:12–16	150
3:7–14	150–151
4:6–8	143
4:13	52, 93

Colossians
1:9–14	81–82
3:1–4	153
3:9–10	158
3:12–17	84

1 Thessalonians
5:23–24	82

1 Timothy
6:11–16	152

2 Timothy
1:7	142
2:10–13	120
4:8	86
4:18	104

Titus
2:11–14	85

Hebrews
2:9	157
4:1	169, 171
4:9–11	141, 169, 171
10:14	135, 169, 171
10:19	162, 169, 172
10:23	169, 172
10:24	170, 172
10:38–39	152
12:1–2; 22–24	80, 162, 170, 172
12:28	170, 172
13:3	111
13:12	159, 161, 173
13:13	170, 173
13:15	170, 173
13:20–21	137

James
1:2–4	120
4:7	119

1 Peter
1:3–9	121
2:24	53
5:5–11	127

1 John

1:7.................... 159, 161

1:9......................... 161

3:1–3..................... 136

4:7–11................ 85–86

4:16....................... 136

Jude

24–25..................... 133

Revelation

3:7–8.............. 111–112

12:11...... 128, 159, 161

About the Author

Derek Prince (1915–2003) was born in India of British parents. He was educated as a scholar of Greek and Latin at Eton College and King's College, Cambridge in England. Upon graduation he held a fellowship (equivalent to a professorship) in Ancient and Modern Philosophy at King's College. Prince also studied Hebrew, Aramaic, and modern languages at Cambridge and the Hebrew University in Jerusalem. As a student, he was a philosopher and self-proclaimed agnostic.

While in the British Medical Corps during World War II, Prince began to study the Bible as a philosophical work. Converted through a powerful encounter with Jesus Christ, he was baptized in the Holy Spirit a few days later. Out of this encounter, he formed two conclusions: first, that Jesus Christ is alive; second, that the Bible is a true, relevant, up-to-date book. These conclusions altered the whole course of his life, which he then devoted to studying and teaching the Bible as the Word of God.

Discharged from the army in Jerusalem in 1945, he married Lydia Christensen, founder of a children's home there. Upon their marriage, he immediately became father to Lydia's eight adopted daughters—six Jewish, one Palestinian Arab, and one English. Together, the family saw the rebirth of the state of Israel in 1948. In the late 1950s, they adopted another daughter while Prince was serving as principal of a teacher training college in Kenya.

In 1963, the Princes immigrated to the United States and pastored a church in Seattle. In 1973, Prince became one of the founders of Intercessors for America. His book Shaping History through Prayer and Fasting has awakened Christians around the world to their responsibility to pray for their governments. Many consider underground translations of the book as instrumental in the fall of communist regimes in the USSR, East Germany, and Czechoslovakia.

Lydia Prince died in 1975, and Prince married Ruth Baker (a single mother to three adopted children) in 1978. He met his second wife, like his first wife, while she was serving the Lord in Jerusalem. Ruth died in December 1998 in Jerusalem, where they had lived since 1981.

Until a few years before his own death in 2003 at the age of eighty-eight, Prince persisted in the ministry God had called him to as he traveled the world, imparting God's revealed truth, praying for the sick and afflicted, and sharing his prophetic insights into world events in the light of Scripture.

Internationally recognized as a Bible scholar and spiritual patriarch, Derek Prince established a teaching ministry that spanned six continents and more than sixty years. He is the author of more than fifty books, six hundred audio teachings, and one hundred video teachings, many of which have been translated and published in more than one hundred languages. He pioneered teaching on such groundbreaking themes as generational curses, the biblical significance of Israel, and demonology/spiritual warfare.

Prince's radio program, which began in 1979, has been translated into more than a dozen languages and continues to touch lives. Derek's main gift of explaining the Bible and its teaching in a clear and simple way has helped build a foundation of faith in millions of lives. His nondenominational, nonsectarian approach has made his teaching equally relevant and helpful to people from all racial and religious backgrounds, and his teaching is estimated to have reached more than half the globe.

In 2002, he said, "It is my desire—and I believe the Lord's desire—that this ministry continue the work, which God began through me over sixty years ago, until Jesus returns."

Derek Prince Ministries persists in reaching out to believers in over 140 countries with Derek's teaching, fulfilling the mandate to keep on "until Jesus returns." This is effected through the outreaches of more than thirty Derek Prince offices around the world, including primary work in Australia, Canada,

China, France, Germany, the Netherlands, New Zealand, Norway, Russia, South Africa, Switzerland, the United Kingdom, and the United States. For current information about these and other worldwide locations, visit: www.derekprince.org